D1215890

SPIRIT LANDS

Sarah Wardle was born in London in 1969. She was educated at Cheltenham Ladies' College; Oxford, where she read Classics; and Sussex, where she read English. She won *Poetry Review*'s new poet of the year award in 1999 and her first collection, *Fields Away* (Bloodaxe Books, 2003), was shortlisted for the Forward best first collection prize. Her second book, *SCORE!* (Bloodaxe Books, 2005), included some of the poems she broadcast while poet-in-residence for Tottenham Hotspur Football Club, as well as the script of a film-poem, 'X: A Poetry Political Broadcast'. *A Knowable World* (Bloodaxe Books, 2009) followed her detainment in a Central London psychiatric hospital. Her most recent Bloodaxe collections are *Beyond* (2014) and *Spiritlands* (2019). She has been a Royal Literary Fund Fellow at Royal Holloway, University of London, and works as a creative writing tutor for Morley College, Westminster Kingsway College and the Workers' Educational Association.

SARAH WARDLE

Spiritlands

BLOODAXE BOOKS

ISBN: 978 1 78037 434 5

First published 2018 by
Bloodaxe Books Ltd,
Eastburn,
South Park,
Hexham,
Northumberland NE46 1BS.

www.bloodaxebooks.com
For further information about Bloodaxe titles
please visit our website or write to
the above address for a catalogue.

Supported using public funding by
**ARTS COUNCIL
ENGLAND**

Cover design: Neil Astley & Pamela Robertson-Pearce.

Printed in Great Britain by Bell & Bain Limited, Glasgow, Scotland, on
acid-free paper sourced from mills with FSC chain of custody certification.

To Aidan Williams
with gratitude and affection

Suddenly snow comes
and enters our lives like love,
shining with wonder.

ACKNOWLEDGEMENTS

Acknowledgements are due to the editors of the following publications in which some of these poems first appeared: *DulwichOnView*, *The Holocaust in History and Memory*, *Morley Magazine*, *The Spectator* and *South Bank Poetry*.

CONTENTS

Song for World

What we need right now is not nationalism,
but a resurgence of animism,
a revival of eco-spirituality,
not the islander mentality,

but the larger view of earth as home
and universe as possession
that all men, just as each thing,
owns by natural law, beginning

with an outlook of coexistence
and simultaneity, acceptance
of every culture, people, place,
living together in tolerance,

everyone starting by improving the manners
he shows to neighbours, colleagues, strangers,
not so much a global outlook,
but inner, outer, local, cosmic,

knowing the world and all things in it
from organisms to the inanimate,
from the still centre, appreciating
being by mindfully meditating

on the existence of what's beyond the self,
not thoughts and moods, but all else,
since only in this way can feeling
be reduced to breath and kin hearts beating.

The Golden Bough

A branch floats downstream on the Thames,
blown in the storm from park, or garden,
and takes on symbolic meaning,
an olive truce, a cherry wedding,
the arm of a Leviathan,
Noah's relief on nearing land,

a message, as in a castaway's bottle,
of life, borne wherever it settles,
and if taking root, evolving
into a cutting, the world revolving
all the while, shoot and growth
leading on from graft and earth,

like ancient Greek city states,
founded by embarking migrants,
or the way that north America
was settled by the Pilgrim Fathers,
or how the African continent
was explored up by European men,

and now how folk travel here,
as tides bring peoples, or birds winter
in another hemisphere to breed,
for as world gives, so it receives,
and while the globe moves, we rotate,
like trade winds around the planet.

Votive

I focus on this Mayan bear,
hiding his eyes behind his paws,
the culture that crafted him
ancient as the civilisation
of Shiva, Anubis, or Ceres,
minded of age-old mysteries,

the Ionian goddess of fruitlike breasts,
Egypt's weighing of the heart at death,
the mandala, zodiac and phoenix,
turtle that holds up the world, the egg
from which the entire cosmos hatched,
Gaia and Ouranos, old Norse giants,

Celtic shields and Druid stone circles,
Lascaux's handprints and hunted animals,
Aztec pyramids, Saxon barrows,
carved bone calendars, once the tomorrows
of Inca and African spirit-times,
all still here in the mind behind his eyes.

Spiritlands

Somewhere by the Tigris
in the Great War my father's father
is the sole survivor, and deeply wounded.
He listens till he knows
he's the last life left on the battlefield
and though pained by the shrapnel
the Turks have just blown in his left side,
he rises, glad to be alive.
And something like will makes him walk on,
though he wants to wretch at the smell
of blood, bodies baking in the sun
on which birds of prey are already feasting.
And all his belief is now leaving him,
yet still he gets up and walks away,
whither he doesn't know,
but in the direction he remembers
there might have been a village
that was spared.
                              At this point
we jump-cut to the Second World War
in Greater London, where my mother's
a toddler who already understands
too much of adult life, how it can
go right, but also very wrong.
Now she is escaping, as she does
most of the time, always running away,
loosening her grip on both parents' hands,
so wilful, worried, wandering off
that her father has built a tall fence
around their garden, which tonight
fails to keep her in, after the air raid
and shelter again, the sirens and bombs
that affected even outer London,
so that she's off, making a getaway,
heading for an idea of safety, far too

young to be supposed to know of life
and death and what all the concerned talk
of the adults is about, but she understands
in her fashion, for this war too
has not yet ended.
                    And on and on
my Victorian grandfather walks
away from the battlefield,
just as on and on my mother
barrels away from her own wartime,
until in wonderment and in a time warp
of sorts, they catch sight of each other,
joyfully meet and smile.

And to my grandfather, my mother is,
a small child venturing out
from her nomadic tribe under a hot sun.
And to my mother, this old man,
who died when I was five, is alive,
not yet her father-in-law-to-be,
nor her own father whom she lost young,
or my father, her future husband,
but to her this soldier is everything
she has been seeking of security and faith,
as she is all the hope and promise
he has been looking for, as he picks her up,
holds her in his arms
and dances, dances, dances,
innocently, tenderly, celebrating peace,
until as it starts to grow dark at the desert's
sudden nightfall, he returns her safely
to her home, her village, her people,
where he is taken in, fed, nursed, given rest,
hospitality, welcome.
                    Soon war will be over.
Never again will he touch a soldier's
rations of plum-and-apple jam,
nor speak of the horrors he has seen,

while Mother will be comforted too
by peace, the sense of mass relief,
tales of street dancing in the city centre
and crowds waving flags for Victory,
yet she'll always be a wise sceptic
on religion, 'God' and happily-ever-after
endings, whilst I like to think
that out there these two are still
trusting in the power of good together,
joyously dancing, dancing, dancing forever,
as at the end of a movie when all is resolved,
normality restored, expansive music
played, then the soundtrack theme again
kicks in one last time, as the camera
zooms out to panorama and a helicopter's
bird's eye view, before the credits roll
and pairs of young lovers emerge
from cinemas down the decades into light.

Amina's Truth

mother sisters brother on fire burn
in my eye now, no english, i learn

third language, trying forget, make friend,
me syrian, here britain women

lots freedom but I wanting return
where husband war, mother die, i born,

she flames, sisters brother shout, bombs kill
most, town skeleton, father fights, will

not live say text, so i come uk
to questions, men, papers, is ok?

i wanting ask what mean? me need show?
see they things i saw? but i not know

words, how explain, so nodding, smiling
time all, my son in arms, and crying

Night Nurses

My heroes are not the ones who kill,
but the everyday kind, like night nurses,
who emerge shining into the day,
as we're just waking. If they're lucky,
they might have snatched a brief break
between doing battle with acute cases
and police arrivals. Or on the rare times
the ward is quiet, they'll still have spent
hours reassuring through tired smiles
the ones who can't sleep. Now they go,
as a next shift comes, fresh with a sense
of work well done, returning home
to their own charges, their husbands
who too need looking after and children
who have learnt to love their softness.
Where are the statues and memorials
for all the heroines who protect us?
I would march for peace and the hand
that holds, not shoots. Isn't it time
these women were also remembered?

First-hand Evidence

In my childhood you could still see them,
bomb-damaged areas, staircases open

like dolls' houses, playgrounds for kids,
bringing to life tales of the Blitz,

like the one my grandmother told of the man
she knew who tracked an enemy plane

on his nightshift, as he watched helpless,
its bomb falling over his own address,

and came home to find everything lost
but his sister's hand, turning the key in the lock.

In the Memorial to the Murdered Jews of Europe

This is art which imitates death,
a stone ocean with roots in men's breath,
a human wound of gas grey cement,
of false hope – Emergency Exit –
the tombs getting deeper further in,
each one thousands of unknown civilians,
a cemetery of inert graves,
drowned in unstable silence, mass waves,
no labyrinth holding hope of a centre,
or way out, each matchbox tile a chamber,
every block tall as a prison wall,
or an army closing in for the kill,
but still the green candles of trees
let in life, like children's birthdays.

The Spirit to Solve

The mosaic of cultures of the world
co-exist in an unsaid dimension.
War brings uncertainty, tragedy, changes of nation.
Life can find our fixed views hurled
into productive, progressive flexibility.
In our rearview mirrors we see receding
all the knowns we thought of and start believing
in the unlikely, unexpected improbability
that rarely things do work out really,
like a mountain pass out of trouble, siege, difficulty,
found by effort, compromise, ingenuity,
a mutual respect for faith in humanity,
a space in our heart of hearts where the random
meets trust, imagination, alliance, compassion.

Human Spirit

I was out of place, luck and mind,
as the city crowds walked on by,
looking right through me, or away.
Nobody smiled, or stopped to say,
'Hello, how are you? Can I help?'
I felt like I was somewhere else,
not a part of the street at all,
that no one would come, if I called.

I'm a whole human too.
Treat me as I would you.

An army of suits marched along.
I thought that I'd never belong
to the mainstream of rush hour.
Commuters' faces looked sour,
as they threw glances, frowns and coins,
but now reading between the lines,
I see they were scared more than me.
I represented poverty,

homelessness and unemployment,
all of the things they had spent
careful lives trying to avoid;
no wonder then some looked annoyed.
I sat there alone and begged,
as though I were society's dregs.
Last leaves were clinging to the trees,
like refugees to old countries.

I'm a whole human too.
Treat me as I would you.

Meanwhile it rained. Snow fell and stuck.
I prayed Allah would bring me luck.
Then I was helped by a stranger,
where the rest saw only danger.
She handed me to the safety
of The Salvation Army.
I was given clothes, food, a room,
hope and medical attention.

Now I've been here for twenty years,
I help others allay their fears,
who don't even know the language,
have just the clothes they wear, no sandwich,
cash, cards, family, friends, or home.
They're lost, vulnerable, alone.
We give them kindness, charity,
a bed, the chance to earn money,

learn English and how to fit in,
offer them a new beginning.
Every time I pass somebody
who's come from another country
and looks as though they're out of place,
I don't see a statistic, or case,
but my younger self in their face
and the whole of the human race.

I'm a whole human too.
Treat me as I would you.

Pamphleteering

Is every literary author another Luther,
exhorting a personal channel to the spirit,
nailing his, or her, pamphlet to a closed door
in the hope it affects any who read it

and that it might change the status quo,
beating a path to calm and logic,
trying to leave an imprint on tomorrow,
beyond self-expression, or rhetoric,

party politics, or organised religion,
trying to disseminate the stillness of being,
as a poet, or playwright, of conviction,
illuminating the sight of inner seeing,

not viewed through the lens of one creed,
but through an understanding of nature,
deeper dimensions, how world is experienced:
subatomic vibrations of morals, mind, matter?

At Dove Cottage

The Wordsworths' grave at Grasmere
is covered by fallen leaves,
while in Dove Cottage his chair
is empty, although it seems

his spirit haunts the houseplace,
a manuscript left open,
as if he'd written the page
just now and then had broken

off to dream into the fire,
which blazes in the old hearth,
bright as daffodils, his ear
measuring verse from the heart,

in silence but for the flames,
calm in which to recollect
powerful feelings, thoughts, rhymes
and exact words to express

overflowing emotion,
as through lattice-window glass
the lake clouds brim and darken
for a storm to come, then pass.

Schoolgirl to Teacher

Where you see revolution and difference,
nation and battlefield, tip and balance,
I'm wondering, imagining, extending
and hazarding how the Greeks and Incas
were just like us. I'm empathising,
abstracting, hypothesising and suggesting
that Elizabethans and Egyptians
were of similar flesh. While you argue
and retract, probe, refute and reject,
I'm intuiting, comparing, generating
and relating how the Bronze Age
and Renaissance were much like today
and if you'll only stop projecting,
analysing and disrupting, you might let
the bones and grave goods, tools, pots
and coin hoards, inscriptions, art
and manuscripts have their say
that they each belonged to people who
worked, ate, slept, sang, danced, fought,
loved and lived in much the same way.

Mr Wales

Unusually for me, I'd signed consent,
was there in my blue surgical socks,
as if on a transatlantic flight,
worried about what I'd embarked on,
face to face with the anaesthetist,
who was ready to insert the catheter,
let the milky drug enter my veins,
when the surgeon, a big, tall rugby
player of a man, now fixed forever
as a father figure, said the procedure
could do more harm than good
and cancelled the operation,
despite the cost, which restored
my faith in the medical profession.

Careless Whisper

The cleaner told me the room I was moving into
had just been vacated by you-know-who,
singer of *Wake Me Up Before You Go Go*,
how he'd had to completely vacuum and shampoo
the carpet after what the star did on it,
all you can think of and vomit, piss, shit.
I've seen other cases of this,
men treating sheets, or shower, as a toilet,
as if they want to be a baby, or invalid.
Some men shave off their hair and eyebrows.
Some throw the furniture around.
I can picture him being rapidly held down,
like a rape scene he never recovered from.
If he was looking for fast love, he got some.
And now we can't wake him up. He's gone.

Art Therapy

A young offender in therapy
paints a boy standing alone on the beach,
arms outstretched in the sign of the Cross,
a portrait of himself on day release,
embracing the wide open, restless as the sea,
as his key worker watches from a café seat.
The frail figure roars against the wind,
feeling free, fresh air on his pale face,
now keeping – not doing – time
with the foaming anger of the waves,
while in the sand his footprints make
graffiti like the art that sent him to jail.

On Empty Street

The street of empty homes rings with the fall
of rain on cobbles and the sink from grace
of a community, where once the tall
helped the weaker to a better place.
Sleet hammers on the corrugated iron
that masks the doors and windows of each house.
Weeds sprout from gutters in this wild ruin,
where social housing goes to rat and mouse.

Once begged to vote for industry and jobs,
the unemployed of this abandoned town
were let down not by reds, but brainless sods
in boardrooms, for whom the merry-go-round
goes on as steely CEOs jump ship,
while ghost-town streets like this that could be filled
with doorbells and washing are Atlantis,
from whose seabed young tree roots have now spilled.

But turn into this side road at full moon
and tricks of mind and light might let you see
the dead marching for rights to an old tune,
sung on the wind and for equality.
There, hung from old chimney pots, a banner
strung like Christmas lights in a southern town,
demands 'Work For All'. Beats of a drummer
here are sent skyward as protesters turn

the corner, brushing past you in the cold,
striding out of the nineteenth century
into the twenty-first, shouts loud and bold,
echoing justice and democracy.
Blink again and this narrow street has changed
back now to its true state of emptiness,
while an empty state leaves child runaways
and those on the streets vulnerable and homeless.

City Rain

When storm and hail assail the sky
and turn the light to shades of grey,
we're each one of the passers-by
in an oil painting, a brushed face

with black umbrella in a street
that could be now or years ago,
the traffic cars, or horse-drawn carts,
while city fashions come and go,

lamps turn from gas to electric,
but all the time, it seems, the rain
hangs overhead, as transatlantic
passages change from boat to plane,

wars are fought and governments fall,
and still the downpour carries on,
uniting pedestrians, all
in Manchester, Paris, London,

stepping on to work and meetings
with the energy of the crowd,
thoughts of pedestrians fleeting,
as if almost uttered aloud

in the whirr of modern living,
with people walking with the flow
and against, and the sky sieving
the day's rain, like the status quo.

Mill-hands Conversing, 1919

(after Winifred Knights)

Outside the mill the women gather
to agitate for equal pay.
A red jacket indicates their leader,
who could be a Labour activist today.
This was a year of nationwide strikes,
that spread like influenza.
There's no crèche, no workers' rights,
so a mother brings her toddler with her.

The war to end all wars has stolen
the dreams of many of these girls,
culled a generation of young men
and left a mutilated world.
Now some women over thirty
are able to exercise their vote.
They speak of rights, equality,
have yet to see how waves of change broke:

full women's suffrage, the next world war,
the NHS and civil rights.
Some things will come good, as before.
They believe in progress, set their sights
on horizons, these sunlit fields and hill,
painted in the background landscape,
while in the foreground the stern mill,
shows that for now there's small escape.

Yet new times are inevitably coming.
A few men stand by at the edge,
some watch from a distance, grumbling,
and others turn their backs and heads.
They have a king, a male prime minister.
Margaret Thatcher and Theresa May
owe these women who met that summer
for the work they did in paving the way.

Still Life

(after Vanessa Bell)

At fifty you painted your mother at eighteen,
two years older than you were when she died.
You dressed her in scarlet, like a young queen,
and made her prettier than in real life,
something about the tilt of her head
and brightness, like make-up, around her eyes,
as if the way you remembered,
not like her aunt's photo, but with a smile
she gave you long after she was dead,
learnt by heart when you were a child.

Later you painted your daughter at this age,
a vase of white flowers, scissors, cotton,
light falling on her face and the book's page,
her mind caught in thought and absorption,
pleased to see her attention engaged
and how your mother still lingered on
in the same knot of hair, same grace,
same sitter's spark of animation
and way the spirit of your own gaze
was keenly focused in one direction.

Umbrella

I can almost remember
listening to Beyoncé
(or was it Rihanna?)
on a rainy day

in New York, or Paris,
thinking of Monet
(no wait, it was Renoir),
the precise way

in 'The Umbrellas',
the artist's gaze
elicits a blushing stare
from a child who plays

with a hoop by her mother
and a girl, 20 if a day,
who carries a shopper,
each pleased, slightly dazed,

feeling he sees only her
in the pouring rain,
as *ella*, *ella*,
repeated to fade.

US

In Washington Trump tightens
border controls and legislation,
while the roots of his free nation
all stem from immigration.
In New York a Wall Street banker
spends billions on a takeover,
while on the sidewalk a wino begs,
his pockets empty as his dregs.

In Connecticut a researcher
develops a new drug for cancer,
while in a hospital a man
learns he's got it from a scan.
In Massachusetts a Harvard scholar
writes a thesis on labor law,
while a Business School postgraduate
types his case study on profit.

In California in Silicone Valley
IT millionaires surf for dates to marry,
while in Hollywood the latest star
divorces because of an affair.
In Iowa an entrepreneur
earns a fortune from his diner,
while his customers become obese
on hash browns, hamburgers and cheese.

In Colorado an eagle flies
down a Rockies mountainside,
while below on the white water
guides hunt tourists to raft the river.
In Texas at the NASA station
an astronaut prepares for mission,
while on a ranch a cowboy stares
up at vast acres of night stars.

Modern Classics

Pizza vendors by the Coliseum,
street painters by the Pantheon,
tour guides addressing the Forum,
these are the modern ancients of Rome.
There goes Cicero with his iPad
and Seneca blogging on what is good.
The Gracchi blend in with the crowd,
while Virgil uploads the *Aeneid*.

Souvenir shops selling vases with gods on,
hotels with a view of the Parthenon,
prove the Agora is still at the heart of Athens,
though the economy's dead as Agamemnon.
Plato posts a selfie with Socrates.
Clouds is shared on the Cloud by Aristophanes.
The web is trending with a new Pericles,
as the same sun rises and sets over Greece.

Artistic Preference

I prefer the Puritan merchants of Protestant art,
the businessmen of bourse, wool house and guild,
to madonnas, or scenery with milkmaids, can't
enjoy populated countryside, want fields
and beaches empty, though like a crowd scene
of Hogarthian revellers, or townsfolk who skate
in secular festivity, or Claude Lorraine dream
of classical heroes in an Arcadian landscape,
or that snow-filled Bruegel of the hunters' return
about the time the vernacular displaced Latin.

Letter to the Third Millennium

Who will be your mayor and king?
What will you pledge allegiance to?
What will be the nature of your sins?
What trades and duties will you do?
What will be your currency?
Will you use candles and firewood?
Will you have a concept of mercy?
Will it be shown unto the good?
What will replace the great cathedral,
cresting the city in midday sun?
What power will you give your people,
prince, priest, pedlar, pedestrian?
Will you grant souls to birds and beasts?
What will your bridges be built from?
Who will be honoured at your feasts?
Will they be held in hall and barn?
Will you sip ale, cider, wine?
What will you put upon your plate?
If all worldly riches could be thine,
what would you give? What have in weight?
What will your doublets, tunics, gowns,
be spun of? Will women wear a veil?
What justice will there be in towns?
What weaponry? Yet chain and mail?
Will you have monks and medicine,
and merchants steeped in enterprise?
Will there be taxes and inflation?
How much will you pay in tithes?
And to whom? Will there be lawyers?
Will there be peasants? Will there be knights?
What kind of men will be your courtiers?
Will they be moral, honest, upright?
Will there be universities?
What will dons be professors of?
Who will your poets' patrons be?
Will they still write of time and love?

At Home with the Celts

I see them by the fire in a hillfort room,
him sipping mead from a flagon,
her forking a flesh-hook into a cauldron

of thick, simmering Irish stew,
wearing the torc that will be in her grave goods
one day along with her combs and tools,

while he's recalling battles, the bellowing horn,
spirals on his shield that gave protection,
faces of men slain and of fortune,

and as she serves up the meaty broth
and he eats of it, comforting and hot,
his frown unknots: a simple truth.

Cassie at Six

Cassandra is in the playground,
holding two pink balloons on strings,
already feeling a little different
from the rest. As she watches the boys
kick a football, she can foresee
who will win, who will lose.
She tries to tell a girl not to climb
the slide, that she will fall,
split her chin open, but the girl
carries on to her fate. She has inklings
of what is to come, a vague sense
of doom, though unaware as yet
of international conflict, war,
being taken by force as prisoner
and concubine, the death of the one
she will have to love and of herself.
Her mother calls her home.
She is already tired of not
being believed, so doesn't say
that supper will be burnt again
and she knows one day her father
will be killed. Instead she takes
a last ride on the roundabout,
caught up in the madness
of its spinning, like the world.

Topspin Theory

If the unknown power that created all
retracted everything to one place
and became merely a tennis ball
which God, a small girl, threw into space
and because of the absence of gravity
spun up into what was left of air
to the field beyond the last galaxy
out in the ghostliness of nowhere,
we could still be certain nonetheless
in the truth that Allah will exist,
that eternal life shall be there for us,
whether in Jehovah, or in Jesus,
just if there were any meaning in it
would be something we might still debate.

Lotus

Let me inhabit this zen
moment of yang and yin.
Like Buddha reclining,
I'm peaceful as the pond
with waterlilies in bloom
and cicadas singing.

My soul is still, has no room
for doubt, or depression,
anger, or agitation.
My origami mind
unfolds in contemplation.
My thoughts become a swan.

My bowl is full to the brim.
My past life is healing.
My next reincarnation
will be as a dragon.
I'm aware of no ending:
there'll always be something.

Dreamtime

Guide us by these painted rocks,
those stones heaped in arrows,

by fallen trunks pointing north
and chalked caves to shallows,

burial sites and landscapes
of dreamtime, familiar shapes,

like that river, or this ridge,
this curved bay, that red cliff,

or the night sky in summer,
constellations, like hunter

and lurcher, the 3D maps
that lead us to spiritlands,

where past, present, future merge
in an open universe

and footprints fade, but our bones
persist in the dust and glow

of the A-Z of stars,
the Facebook of ancestors.

Abigail's Wedding

As you come down the aisle on the arm of your father
outside in the grounds of the old house,
the sun starts to shine through and mid-summer
keeps clouds from opening, while your spouse
waits in robes for you to walk seven times
around him under a canopy of white,
and as a glass breaks, rings are exchanged, page signed,
some of us gathered here have tears in our eyes.
So now may you both have a bright future
and good fortune follow you down the years
with life that henceforth goes smoother,
dispelling past anxiety and fears,
as on this day, like Moses parting waves,
somewhere God is keeping rain at bay.

Amanda

When I didn't recognise the number
and saw the text with kisses, but no name,
'Thinking of you: they're playing *Native New Yorker*',
I racked my brain and was filled with shame.
Was this the divorced father and one-night stand,
or was this someone who had heard me sing
in hospital when I was out of my mind,
or was this a teenage flame rekindling?
And then I was relieved to realise
it was not a blast from the past, but you
who heard me play that record in the seventies
when we were small, who shared with me and knew
my childhood home, pets, dad and mum,
yet lost your own mother, aged so young.

Blue Rosette

You stand there making a hustings speech:
law and order, defence, foreign policy.
I'm in blue again. It's '83.

You hold your head high as a general.
Like a pop song, you raise the tempo,
building to an eve-of-poll crescendo.

I spot the familiar jokes and themes.
My life is canvassing, Latin and Greek.
I'm in a pinstriped dress. I'm 13.

I don't question that Tories do it best.
I look up to you, without knowing it yet.
So far I haven't thought about death,

how chimpanzees mourn their leader.
I've been pictured in the *Bexhill-on-Sea Observer*
and am the voice on your car's loudspeaker,

exhorting the whole constituency
to support the Conservative Party,
but I'm too young to vote, Daddy.

I will always elect you unopposed.
Now a box holds your manifestos,
a cross becomes my kiss for the man they chose.

Out on the Hustings, 1974

It was a year of two elections.
Was it February, or October then,
when out canvassing, aged four,
with my maternal grandmother,
a North Stanmore councillor,
Jeremy Thorpe, the leader
of the old Liberal Party,
spotted a photo opportunity?

I undid my coat in mock anger,
to show my dress: 'We're not your colour!'
Later he was tried at the Old Bailey
on charges of conspiracy
and incitement to murder,
making my political banter
and small child's gut reaction
seem like a wise premonition.

Oxfords of the Mind

How many other Oxfords are there really?
Those in heads of ghosts down centuries,
past, present, future, fourth dimension,
Union, Bod, bar, hall, collection?
Each time Michaelmas approaches,
memories of red ivy, rowing coaches
and sherry fill the air with promise,
chapel and bicycle bells. The mist

has lifted on our imagined future,
yet a shared youth of architecture
and armchair morals magnetise
each gaudy year back to Turl and High.
I glimpse us all still decades on,
like a geriatric Magdalen reunion,
who rise at five to run round the deer park,
trying to reignite that fresher spark,

while a new cohort matriculates,
other minds resuscitate the fates
and furies, Sappho, Solon, Caesar,
and a few dream of being a writer,
ending up with a Collected Works,
like a headstone, their lines in quotation marks
in tutorial essays and finals scripts,
subject of posthumous debates among critics.

In one Oxford is a postgrad making coffee,
while midnight chimes its closing beat,
as he writes his thesis on 'Time in Poetry'
and thinks of a way epistemology
might be used to conclude rhyme is temporal
and spatial at once, both ephemeral
and eternal, written and read on a spectrum,
referencing his imagined self in this poem?

Autumn Effect at Argenteuil

I want to fix the lit moment that now
and again now shines through September trees,
scattering sun on water. At the prow
of my studio boat, I catch the turning leaves,

reflected in the river, how the smoke
from the factory tower blends with the clouds,
juxtaposed with church steeple, where the hope
of the small suburban town prays skywards.

Crowds at the exhibition might assume
this work was rushed *en plein air*, like a sketch,
but I will put more than one afternoon
into the look of ease. What it will fetch

when it is sold is not my main concern.
I'm after a photographic likeness
of light at the cresting of a season,
the frame of a zoetrope, the brightness

of a high sky. I want viewers to feel
how it is now to see out of my eyes,
to be sure banks and horizon were real,
to know that this is how the land here lies

in early autumn of our century,
church and chimney, how industrialised
life turns secular, like the turning leaves,
how art and honesty is what I prize.

Spirit Horse

No need to kick you on.
Now you are the one
guiding me, as we canter
through old landscapes,
riding to the other world
to revisit the ones who died.
You don't stop for grass,
but speed, as if heading

for home. I see the father
my mother lost young;
the grandfather I briefly knew,
holding me on his lap;
then my old dog, chasing
across wheat fields; finally
both grandmothers, letting me
kiss them goodbye. I don't

want to think that this place
will one day hold my parents,
aunt, uncle, that at length
it will contain my love and me.
And just as I'm feeling this,
you pick up on it and turn,
as I used to sense your fear
at a motorbike, the engine

that made you startle and tense
beneath me, and you bear me
back here to the present,
letting me dismount, take off
your tack, loose you out
into the field one last time.
I can still feel the shape
of your saddle even now.

Midlander

My spirit is still in Salop and Staffs,
where I grew up through years of daffs
with the easy way that people talked,
slow and sing-song, fields to walk
to notice a frosted spider's web,
fallen acorns, crab apples, a hedge

for blackberry picking, seas of wheat,
the conscious chatter of a stream
and rabbit holes, somewhere a warren,
like the mind's ways, complex, hidden,
that take me back down bridleways,
over stubble, past bales of hay,

on lanes that will always lead to home,
to honeysuckle, a house, a garden,
where spade and fork are, a hose is,
and somewhere Mother pruning roses,
where my father was truly happy,
drinking in the view of the valley.

I remember hills weren't blue, but green,
the Sheepwalks flecked with flocks, still see
the great, black arch at Ironbridge span
the gorge, like a lifeline on my hand,
and how the Severn would flow on
to points beyond a child's horizon,

recall the Albrighton Woodland,
the way a trotting pony quickened
to a canter, how to lean into a jump,
the smell of horses' sweat and dung,
pungent as a field of Kentish hops,
but sweeter, bearings that I lost

when we moved south, where the snow
rarely settles and what I know
of No Man's Green and Gilbert's Cross
is otiose, though never lost,
the roads to Bridgnorth, Enville, Kinver,
though these will stay with me forever,

here worthless as an old pound note.
I heart the Midlands as lamb, or foal,
attaches to its ewe, or mare,
or a potato turns up where
you dig and shake the clay soil from it,
with roots that go deep. Honest.

And if you ask me, *What is Birmingham?*
I'd tell you that to me it's learning and
I mean by this not exams and books,
but how to dive in the swimming pool,
not philosophy, or how to think,
but how to fall in the ice rink,

not a degree in English Literature,
but going to the Hippodrome to see Shakespeare,
not science, but the art of skipping
in a group, or taking turns skidding
down a hill on a school-dinner tray,
or how to act in your first play,

perform a Grade I piano piece,
recite a poem to an audience
that gets you by heart, stays with you forever,
make friends who last when you're older,
knowing not to cheat, lie, or steal,
along with spelling and times tables,

not physics, but your first shot at goal,
first sleepover away from home,
when it was simple and the most crazed
it got was the Bull Ring and Five Ways,
when you knew New Street was a name,
but before you'd ever taken the train

alone to London, or up to Glasgow,
before life became a fast show,
when you could sit beneath a playground tree
and watch the daylight through the leaves,
illuminating something more than knowledge,
not the texts they make you read in college,

but the feeling of knowing you're alive
under a Midlands sun and skies
in the heart of the nation, at the still centre
of your mind, grounded, at midday, mid-year,
when you wrote on a schoolbag name, address,
country, continent, world and universe.

On Connecting

The question I'm taking for my thesis
is how can we in a metropolis
relate to rock, tree, spring, stream, sod,
without positing only one God,

and how can we resuscitate
our human need to fabricate
spirits for wood, river, rainbow, well,
to visualise below the soil as hell,

or Hades, and sky as heaven, to understand
the land as harbinger of hope that demands
winter in return for spring,
not deserved guilt, or predestined sin,

but through the workings of the universe,
Gaia as good witch, grandmother earth,
when we're offline and Nature's web
needs refreshing, when we're disconnected

from agriculture and butchery,
from the roots of our psyche's history,
in order to live better in our souls,
reinvigorate bones, blood, cells,

unless we consciously attempt to feel
the coexistence of country and city
and explore the bens, dales, vales, glens,
burns, braes, spinneys, copses, twittens,

or at the very least remember
our common memory via literature,
experiencing Arcadia vicariously
and the *genius loci* through poetry?

Howling Wolf

longs for a snowfall three feet deep,
nocturnal walks across empty fields,
shrill cries of rabbits, killed by stoats,
owls' hunting hoots, warnings of crows,
for the ghost music of the west wind,
lullaby of leaves whispering,
that gold disc balanced on the horizon,
as the day is rising, setting,
and not just when the high noon sun
crests concrete, glass and steel mountains,

but most of all the full moon's spotlight,
female rhythm of a month's nights
that regulates sleep and waking,
not streetlamps' constant glare, breaking
the habit of an adult life
to rest sound and well, sleep deep and tight,
but pitch of dark side, or crescent times,
which enables her to dream blind,
not see further than her hands,
yet visit distant spiritlands.

Soraya and the Spider

A long time ago the world began.
From darkness it was poured.
At length our clever creature, man,
had it all mapped and explored.

The human race rushed about,
hurrying this way and that,
inventing fire, the wheel and doubt,
finding out if the earth was flat.

Mankind built schools and hospitals,
offices, banks and cities,
caused poverty and other ills,
global warming and disease.

He even built a nuclear bomb
which could wipe out his species,
but somehow man knew it was wrong,
so he made war, but also treaties.

He made useful things like mobile phones,
microwaves, cars and computers,
and other things like ice cream cones,
high heels, ties and scooters.

He even created the internet
and the information on it
in each tongue, from England to Tibet,
till it came to hold all knowledge.

But when at length the world wide web
held all there was to be known,
suddenly it developed a giant head
and body of arachnid form.

The online encyclopaedia
had developed an enormous brain.
A big scary tarantula
appeared, as if from a drain.

Its abdomen spanned the whole globe.
Beneath it, we humans cowered.
Eight legs caused tsunamis as it strode.
We truly feared its power.

It said, 'You humans think you're great.
In fact you're very tiny.
Soon you'll be dinner on my plate.
I'll swallow you in my tummy.

You'll be sucked up into a black hole
with the universe and replaced.
The virtual world is now what's real.
You're banished to cyberspace.'

So spoke the spider. And one by one
from Eskimos to Ethiopians,
it gobbled until it had almost eaten
every single one of us humans.

The Canadians were aperitifs.
Then it ate every American,
each Arab, Indian and Chinese,
Australian and African.

But there remained in Bangladesh
a young girl called Soraya.
'I have a theory I'll put to the test.
It's a trick of mind over matter.'

So under a catalpa tree,
Soraya carried out her plan.
She sat very meditatively
and calmly thought, *I am.*

And her act of concentration,
even though she was a child,
sent the spider into consternation
and drove its consciousness wild.

Its brain couldn't cope with the concept
and suffered a synaptic shock.
If Soraya existed, it had to accept
Soraya was, but it was not.

So the world wide web returned
to its proper place in the aether.
But now humankind had learned
to appreciate life and nature,

make sure to get up from his screen,
open windows that are real,
go outside his front door and see
the sun and trees, to think and feel.

So next time you can't keep awake
as you work at a computer station,
think of Soraya, take a break
and be glad for all creation,

every single tree and flower,
each person, face and place,
and be thankful to Soraya
for saving the human race!

May Morning

We wake at Beltane, summer's eve,
to chat about cycles of life.
Who would think, far less believe,
you and I could be a wife

in all the senses of the word
to a man now? Yet our blood runs.
Though most consider it absurd
both of us could still have children

of our own flesh, it's not unheard
that women of our elder age
can conceive and go on to bear
a boy, or girl, or twins. A page

is not filled till the last full stop
of the final chapter's written.
Like good witches, we stir a cup
of nettle tea with cinnamon,

discussing donor eggs and odds
of safely having a live birth,
picture young turned into swans,
inheriting and walking the earth.

May Sunday

May I hold a May moment,
when birdsong and a plane
form a backing track to sun,
lighting leaves like candles
that shine in the cathedral,
as bells summon to prayer,

cascading like a waterfall,
and we lie with each other,
talking about a christening,
planning how to get there
and how much it will cost,
when a helicopter buzzes

like a wasp around a glass,
as voices spill in the street
and a text pings an inbox,
while a dog starts to bark
to the dialogue of children,
as a family's car doors slam

and a motorcycle is revving,
as branches surge in a breeze,
rising like a chest breathing,
sighing like waves sweeping,
while morning is glistening
and a crow beginning to call,

and a jogger's footsteps run,
just as we commit to going
and the foliage lifts like sails
on the verge of setting off
across a measureless ocean,
and all is full, green and alive?

Reminiscence at the Community Centre

As Edna reminisces
            about the couture gowns she sewed,
along with her own wedding dress
            and outfits for the bridesmaids,
and Anne remembers rice and peas
            and Caribbean blue,
and Fred recalls his motorbike,
            the Great Smog of '52
and the year the Government brought in
            a maximum working week,
and Ivy's face lights up
            at Stewart Granger on the screen,
and Janice goes back
            to Worthing and when Brighton had two piers,
while George relives
            flying over France in the war,
I'm thinking of
            the sex you and I had an hour ago,
wondering how
            your fleet are faring as they flow
up through the nooks and crannies
            of my forty-something body
and whether they'll make
            a safe D-Day landing in Normandy.

Making

On these long, fruitful days, the rioja
which captures the sun of other Julys,
is relaxing us, as is the summer,
into this unwinding and earthy wine,
into sex on the hoof, on the sofa,
the Persian rug on the sitting room floor,
in the hall, the kitchen by the cooker,
up against the fridge, by the cupboard door,
so I turn down the steaks as they sizzle
and prevent potatoes boiling over,
just as we turn up the heat, then simmer,
get down to some sugar-icing drizzle,
as if the baby we're trying to make
were spontaneous as a lemon cake.

Kissing in English

As if suspended, held in amber,
so in our lips' taste of cider
is a pippin orchard's summer,
where a field's slope meets a river
and you'll find we all retire,
even in a city rush hour,
back past haystacks to each gold shire,
that is home now and forever,
cuckoo to combine harvester,
ladybird to far Spitfire.

After Astrup

As if a woodcut could be made
of every life and slowly filled
with different emphases, shades,
could we in middle age still
alter the way the picture seems,
like a painter adding touches,
so that by colouring in dreams
we could do ourselves justice,
where the hills were once grey
let in green, a meadow, flowers,
turn an inked night into day
and faceless figures into lovers,
bring a vague foreground on
from lines to sunlit, family home?

On Woodland

I'm usually inclined to be kind
but believe in good over self-interest.
Each time I visit the woods, I'm struck
by world's connectedness, how all is
one system, the way leaves burst out
in photosynthesis, the precise song
of nightingale, tree pipit, warbler,
coexistence of rowan, birch, hazel,
with lichen, moss and ferns, of moth,
dragonfly, white admiral with badger,
squirrel, stoat, and how the whole
flourishes through every living thing
doing what it must, so that I trust
in more than any one single part,
am taken beyond individualism
to the heart of what inhabits habitat.
I've heard tell a man was murdered
in these woods, but all here speaks
of life's renewal, the decomposition
into green. Sometimes I feel afraid,
as if I've gone too far, trespassing
in a universe that grows heedless
of human concerns. Yet I knew
a grandfather who was buried here,
where anemones and bluebells rise
from the cold, dark earth that fathers
forth another spring. There was no
space left in the churchyard for him,
so he was laid to rest where April
is older than Easter and he can take
the long road to ascend to clear skies,
like this one above today, that calls us
over the threshold into another year,
where selfish acts behave like gravity,
but woods are more than sums of trees.